THE BOOMEF INFORMA BOOK

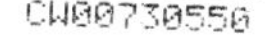

ıis edition first printed in 2001 by JB Books Pty Ltd.

ɛprinted in 2006,2007 by Gecko Books
) Box 118, Marleston, SA 5033

ıthor: Ian King, with thanks to Joseph Morgan from Anuaka Arts.
oduced by: Phoenix Offset, Hong Kong
ɔver Design by: Robert Moller

ıtional Library of Australia,
ıtaloguing-in-Publication

ng, Ian (Ian George), 1954 –
ıe Boomerang Information Book.

BN 0977511421

1. Boomerangs. I. Morgan, Joseph. II. Title.

)9.20282

TABLE OF CONTENTS

INTRODUCTION	3
DREAMTIME – THE BOOMERANG	5
TYPES OF BOOMERANGS	
– Returning	7
– Hunting	9
– Club	11
– Hooked	12
DISTRIBUTION OF BOOMERANGS	14-15
– Y-shaped	16
– U-shaped	17
– X-boomerang	18
BOOMERANG THROWING & CATCHING INSTRUCTIONS	20-21
BOOMERANG ASSOCIATIONS (International)	22-23
DO YOU KNOW?	24-25
THROWING TECHNIQUES	27
ASSOCIATED HUNTING IMPLEMENTS	28

INTRODUCTION

Most of us tend to associate Australia with one type of boomerang, the returning variety. It is generally accepted that the returning type was a later addition to boomerangs.

Origins of a throwing stick are known in Egypt and parts of South America, but it was the Australian Aborigine who created a wide variety of boomerangs that had different applications, thus providing the greatest diversity.

The earliest known evidence has been found at Wyrie Swamp in South Australia dating back to c.10,000 years. This has been scientifically proven by radiocarbon dating. As you read through this book you will begin to appreciate that the boomerang is more than just a toy.

The word boomerang is believed to derive from the Aboriginal word "BOOMORI", although there are different Aboriginal words for the boomerang, this one was eventually anglosized to the boomerang.

The contents of this book is designed to provide the reader with a general overview of the different types of Boomerangs and their relevant applications.

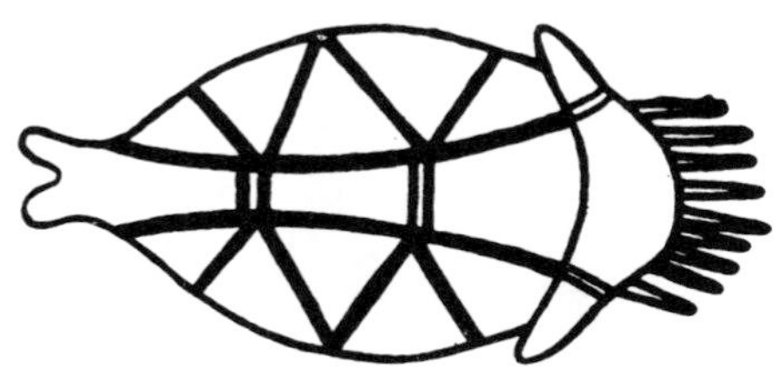

DREAMTIME

The Boomerang that made Night and Day

In the beginning of time the world was lighted by the fire of Bila, the sun woman. On this fire Bila would cook her victims, the Euro-people. One day her dogs killed all of the Euro-people and dragged them back to her camp.

Greatly angered that their neighbours were killed, Kudna - the lizard-man, and Muda - the gecko-man, decided to confront her and seek revenge.

As the two men approached Bila's camp, she took up her boomerang to attack them, but she was too slow. Kudna threw one of his boomerangs at her, causing her great damage. She then turned into a great ball of fire and disappeared. The world was plunged into darkness.

Terrified by the darkness, Kudna and Muda decided to throw their boomerangs into the sky to see if they could bring back the light. Kudna threw one of his boomerangs into the north sky, but no light appeared. Muda threw his to the south, and then into the west, but still no light. Kudna threw again, this time into the east sky. A great ball of fire appeared in the east, slowly rolling across the sky and settling in the west. *Night and day were created.*

RETURNING BOOMERANG

THE RETURNING BOOMERANG

Contrary to popular belief, the Returning Boomerang was not the first type of boomerang used by Aborigines. In fact, this type has only been around for about 200 years. The returning boomerang is best known for its ability to fly in a wide curve and return to its thrower.

Originating in New South Wales, it then made its way to South Australia and Central Australia. With its immense popularity, it is now known world-wide as a symbol of Australia. The main functions of this boomerang were for sport, amusement and the display of the thrower's skill. It was also utilised to a small extent for the purpose of hunting. By throwing the boomerang above the hunted game, it would then drive the flocks into an area better suited for their capture. Some tribes would string nets between trees. As a flock of birds approached the net, a boomerang was thrown high above them as tribesmen made the sound of a hawk.

Fooled by the boomerang imitating a hawk, the birds flew into the nets to avoid the enemy. In doing so many of the birds became entangled in the nets.

In recent years the throwing of returning boomerangs has become recognised as a competitive sport. Competitions are held in various countries each year.

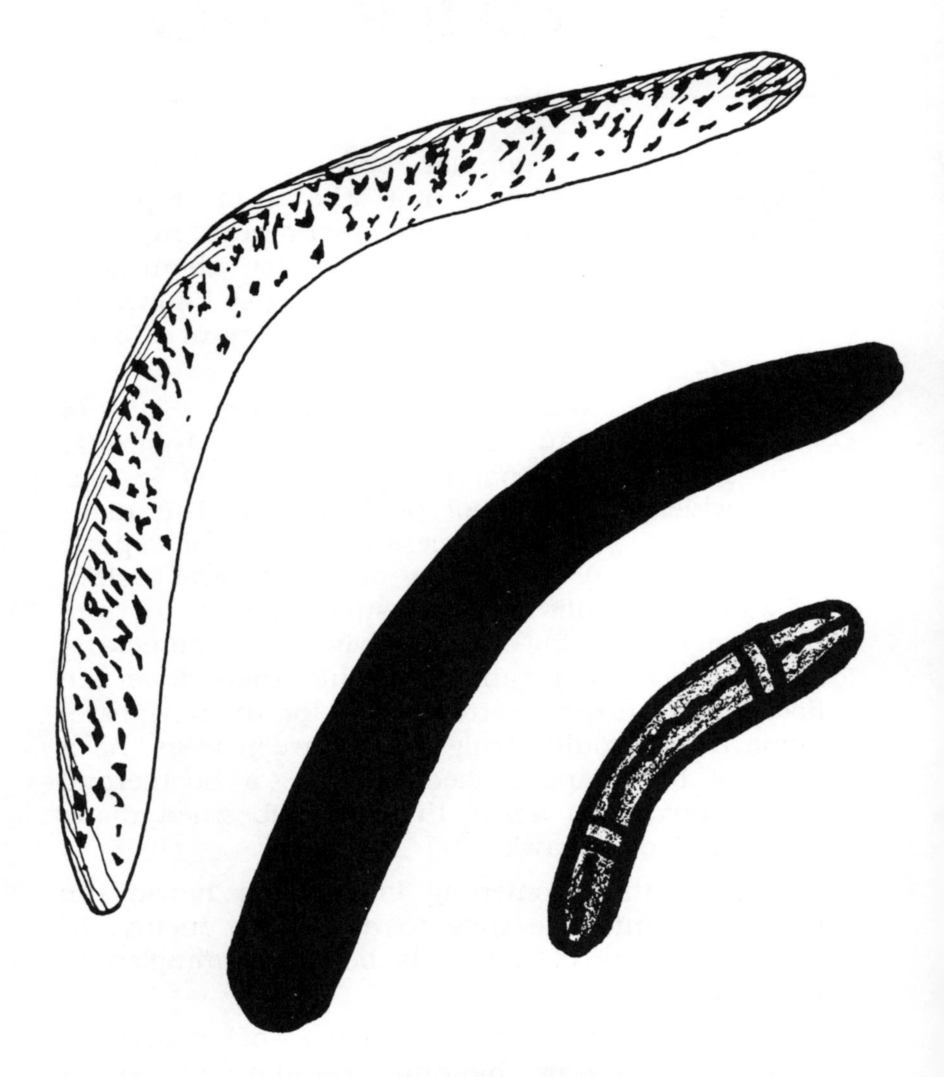

HUNTING BOOMERANG

THE HUNTING BOOMERANG

The Hunting Boomerang is as interesting as the people it served. It's uses are wide and varied, and to the Aborigines it was a highly prized possession. It is a non-returning boomerang and as such, its ability to kill was outstanding.

Not only was this boomerang used to hunt game, but it could be used to create fire, as a digging implement and as a musical instrument.

At a corroboree this boomerang would be used with another one, "clapping" them together to accompany song and dance. They could also be tapped on rocks or the ground, or simply drawn across one another to provide a distinct sound.

This boomerang could be thrown in many different ways. It could be thrown horizontally to the ground with great force, skipping off the ground making it difficult for those on the receiving end to know which direction it would take.

In warfare, the boomerang had the ability to cause severe wounds and in some cases, death would result. Some of these boomerangs would measure up to two metres in length and when thrown at an animal, had the capability to break the legs of its prey.

Although used in warfare, this boomerang's most common use was in hunting food. It would be thrown into a flock of birds with the chance of bringing down more than one, very possible. It's versatility to dig for water, clear fire sites, unearth honey ants and lizards, cut open animals and chop them up, and to scrape hot ashes from baked animals, made it invaluable.

As with other boomerangs, this one was also dependant upon the shape of the root of a tree to give it strength and shape. In Central Australia, Mulga Wood was most commonly used. In other areas, Black Wattle, Bat Willow, Needlewood or Mangrove were the choice wood.

Depending on the area, boomerangs from these regions are painted with ochre, decorated with incised designs representing totemic clans and travels of spirit-heroes, or simply left in the natural state.

CLUB BOOMERANG

The Club Boomerang, being unique in its own design, is similar to the Hunting Boomerang and has a similar shape to the Hooked Boomerang.

This boomerang could be likened to the hammer in some ways, a very strong weapon used in warfare. This boomerang could inflict severe injury onto the person on the receiving end. Not only could it disable an opponent in combat, it could also be used in the clubbing of animals.

Thrown in a similar fashion to the hunting boomerang, the results are similar.

The Club Boomerang was widely used by Aboriginals throughout most parts of Australia.

It's shape was dictated by the root system of the tree it was carved from.

The club head would vary in size and would have to be shaped in such a way to provide balance when used.

The weapon may be decorated with ochre, incised, or simply left in its natural state.

HOOK BOOMERANG

If there was a boomerang that could be classified as a true fighting weapon, the Hooked Boomerang would be it.

It's unusual shape is based on pure sense. In warfare, the Aboriginals would use this boomerang as a means of exposing his opponent, who would be using a shield for protection. The boomerang would "hook" onto the opponent's shield and once this was done, the shield could be pulled from the hands of the person holding it.

Another way of using it was to actually throw the boomerang at close quarters, letting it go as it hooked onto the opponent's shield. It would then pivot on the shield in an arc, hitting the person behind the shield, momentarily disabling him.

"Hooked" boomerangs are generally used in the central regions of Australia and parts of New South Wales.

A hard wood is chosen for this boomerang and it's shape is determined by the tree root. It would be decorated by carving, or with ochre paint.

Unique in it's design, the Hooked Boomerang was a warrior's most chosen weapon.

The Hooked Boomerang could be used to dig small animals and bush tucker from the ground. As with all boomerangs, each have a distinct function.

Once cut and shaped from the tree, and by using a stone axe or similar implement, this boomerang could be tempered over a fire, making it extremely hard. It's edge could be sharpened and in some cases, would actually be used to cut the carcass of an animal into different segments.

Great care was taken to produce this boomerang, because of its many and different uses.

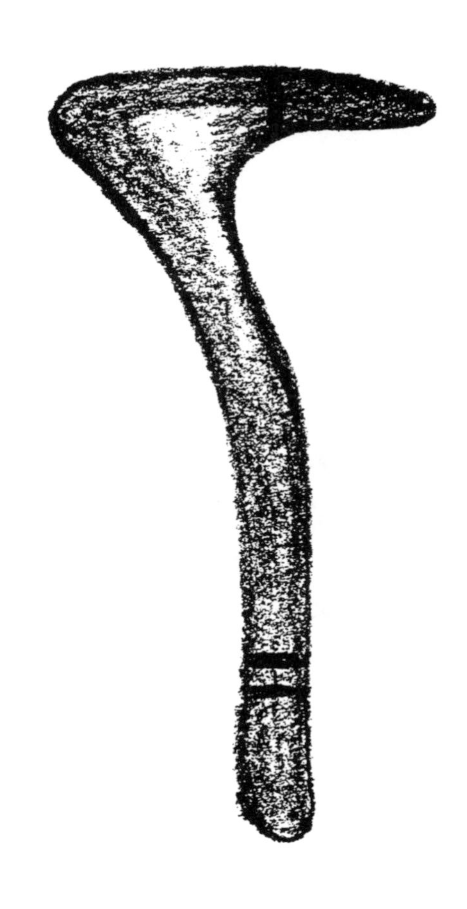

DISTR
OF BOO

CLUB BOOMERANG

HUNTING BOOMERANG

RETURNING BOOMERANG

Returning — Non-returning Boomerangs made.

Boomerangs not made.
(received by trade in some areas)

Non-returning Boomerangs only.

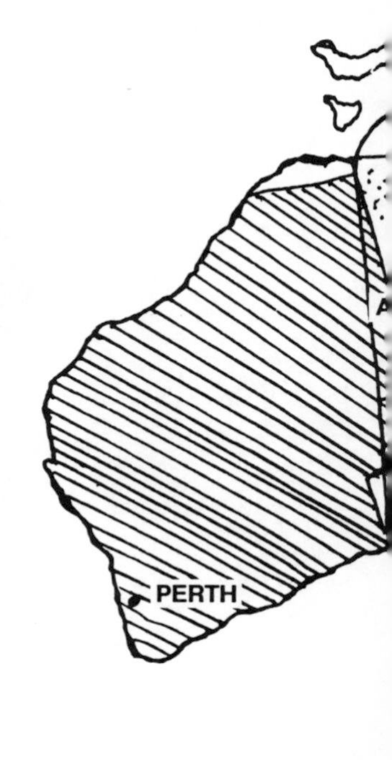

HC

UTION
ERANGS

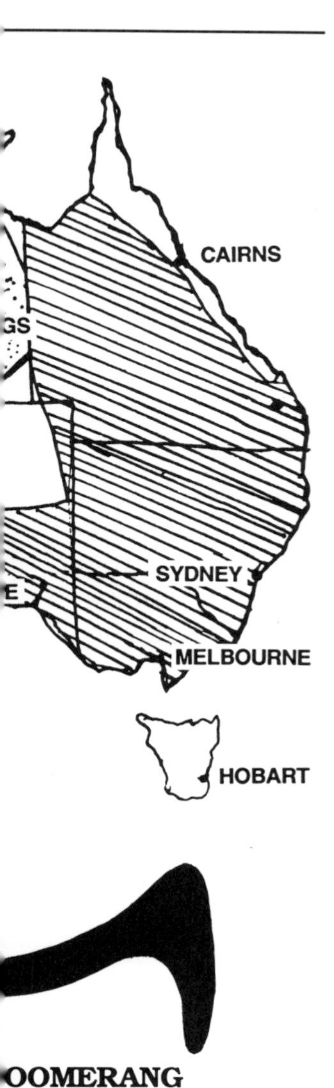

OOMERANG

"U" SHAPED BOOMERANG

CROSSED BOOMERANG

"Y" SHAPED BOOMERANG

"Y" SHAPED BOOMERANG

This boomerang is found most commonly in the Far North Queensland region and is very distinct in its appearance.

It is a fairly recent addition to the range of boomerangs which exist today.

This boomerang is designed to return to the thrower and it can only be made from the right shape of the tree root.

The development of this boomerang goes back some ten years to those Aborigines who live in the Cairns region of Queensland.

In throwing this boomerang the thrower must grab one of the forks. Its effect apart from returning, could be devastating if it were to hit prey at the right point i.e. its stem could plunge into its intended victim, similar to a spear or knife.

When you look at this boomerang you will appreciate its distinctions from all others.

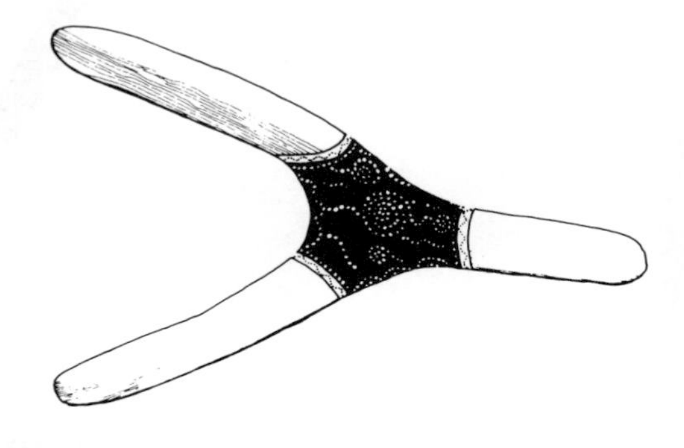

"U" SHAPED BOOMERANG

This boomerang is very distinctive in appearance. Unlike the Returning Boomerang, this type is a "U" shape, but has similar properties to the Returning Boomerang.

It is native to the Far North Queensland region, being flat on one side and rounded on the other surface.

This boomerang is made from Black Wattle and its flight pattern is generally shorter than the wider design of a traded boomerang.

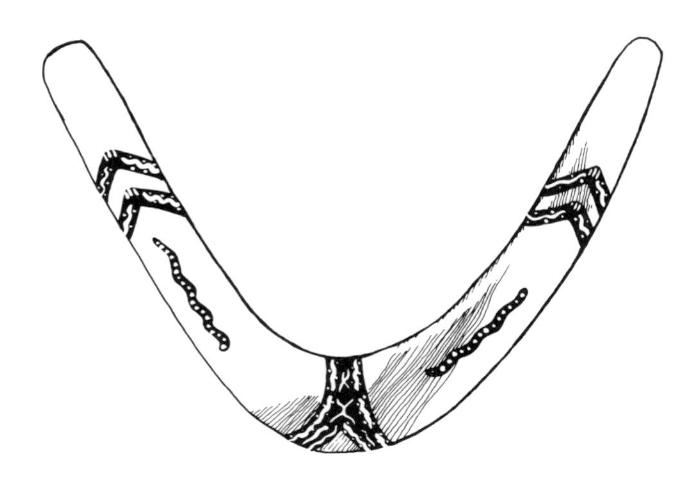

CROSSED BOOMERANG

This boomerang is another variation of the Returning Boomerang, but distinctive in appearance. The Cross Boomerang is from the Tully region of North Queensland. It is a returning boomerang and is painted with varied patterns of the region it comes from.

The boomerang is two pieces of Wattle Wood, approximately one-and-a-half inches wide and eighteen inches long. Each piece is crossed and bound together at the centre using bees wax. The wax is left in the sun to make it pliable, then bound around the boomerang and left to cool and harden.

The art work on these boomerangs is generally painted from earth pigment, and when thrown makes an attractive sight as it spins through the air.

It was used in competitions to see which of the men using it was the most skilled at returning the boomerang to its thrower.

The crossed boomerang is not found anywhere else in Australia.

THROWING INSTRUCTIONS

1. Select a large, clear, grassy area.
2. Hold the boomerang with the flat side to the palm, with the end about the middle of the palm, being held by the thumb and first two fingers. The tip of the boomerang will then rest on the top of your third finger.
3. Raise the boomerang above the shoulder (you will need to throw your boomerang 45 degrees to the right of the wind flow, opposite for a left-handed thrower).
4. Throw the boomerang straight forward (vertical). Do not throw it flat (horizontal). The boomerang should leave your hand in the vertical position and it will right itself as it commences its turn. It will return to you spinning in the flat or horizontal position.

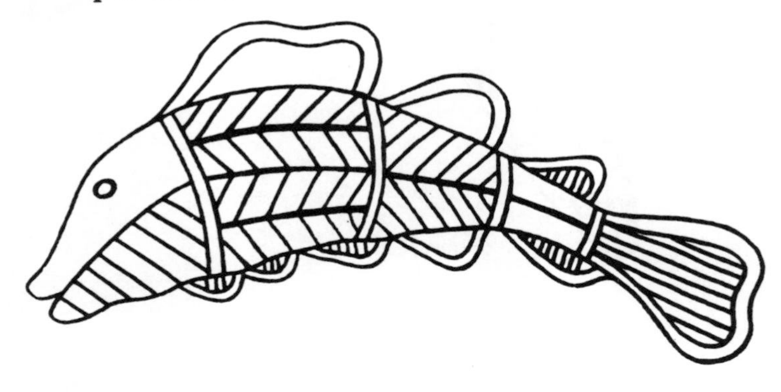

CATCHING THE BOOMERANG

1. Hold your hands open and then clasp your palms together like a book, "sandwiching" the boomerang.
2. Catch only at shoulder level or waist height. Do not try to catch at face or eye level.
3. Do not try to catch a boomerang against the body. Catch with both hands still following the flight-path to the side of the body.
4. Never try to catch the boomerang with one hand, unless you are an experienced catcher.

CAUTION

1. Never throw a boomerang in a strong wind. If the wind is blowing at more than five miles per hour, do not attempt to throw it at all.
2. If it looks like a boomerang might hit you, turn your back, bend over and cover your head.
3. Only one person should throw a boomerang at a time.
4. If a boomerang's flight is interrupted by hitting an object, it will fall to the ground. A boomerang will not return to the thrower after it hits it's target.

BOOMERANG ASSOCIATIONS

AUSTRALIA
Boomerang Association of Australia,
42 Kingswood Drive,
DINGLEY, VICTORIA 3172.

CANADA
Canadian Boomerang Association,
P.O. Box 9331,
STONEY CREEK, ONTARIO, L8G 4F1.

ENGLAND
British Boomerang Society,
9 Bowood Drive,
WOLVERHAMPTON, ENGLAND WV69AW.

FRANCE
Boomerang Club de France,
24 Rue Tronchet,
LYON, FRANCE.

GERMANY
Deutscher Bumerang Club,
Bruckenstrasse 24,
5500 TRIER, W. GERMANY.

BOOMERANG ASSOCIATIONS

HOLLAND
P.O. Box 509, 1180 AM,
Am STEIVELLEN, HOLLAND.

JAPAN
Japanese Boomerang Association,
c/o Afanogawa General Hospital,
83 Konaka - Michinaka,
KANAZAWA CITY,
IGHIKAWA - KEN, JAPAN 920.

SWITZERLAND
Swiss Boomerang Association,
63 Rt. de Chenc,
GENEVA, SWITZERLAND.

UNITED STATES
U.S. Boomerang Association,
1882 Columbia Rd. N.W.,
WASHINGTON D.C., U.S.A. 20009.

DO YOU KNOW?

SOME UNUSUAL FACTS/DID YOU KNOW?

The greatest number of consecutive two handed catches is 801 by Stephane Marquerite of France in 1989.

The longest out and return distance is one of 134.2 meters by Jim Youngblood (USA) in 1989.

The longest flight duration (with self catching) is one of 2 minutes 59.94 sec. by Denis Joyce (USA) in 1989.

Matthiew Weber (Switzerland) caught 73 boomerang throws in 5 min in France 1991.

The number of consecutive catches with two boomerangs, keeping at least one aloft at all times is 207 by Michael Girvin (USA).

Most people tend to think that the throwing boomerang must be held with the concave edge forward, but boomerangs can be held at either end without affecting the flight path.

Boomerangs or throwing sticks were found in excellent condition at the tomb of TUTANKHAMUM EGYPT (1371-1325BC) many of which were capped with gold.

You do not need a strong wrist to impart a spin on a boomerang. This is done by locking the index finger around the boomerang so that as it leaves the thrower, it will pivot over the finger thereby generating the necessary spin required.

You do not need a breeze in order to throw a boomerang, in fact no breeze is more desirable as the boomerang will not have to be adjusted by the thrower to compensate for throwing into the wind.

A short wingspan of a boomerang will create a faster spinning motion and a shorter flight path.

A wide wingspan of a boomerang will cause it to spin slower but a greater distance is created. There are numerous factors such as design, weight, weather condition which will affect overall performance of the boomerang.
There have been many different materials used in the construction of boomerangs such as perspex, ivory, marine ply, fibreglass, nylon, whale bone, metal, polystyrene and a myriad of different woods, all of which will fly provided that the construction and weight factors fall within certain specifications to enable the boomerang to be thrown imparting a spin creating a flight path back to the thrower.
It is possible to throw a boomerang by holding it at the elbow, this can only be done with a small boomerang. A strong grip is needed to impart the required spin.
The worlds oldest Boomerang were found in a peat bog near Millicent South Australia in 1975 and are between 8000 and 10,000 years old. Returning boomerangs are primarily for sport. Hunting and battle boomerangs weigh between 1 and 2 kg.

THROWING TECHNIQUES

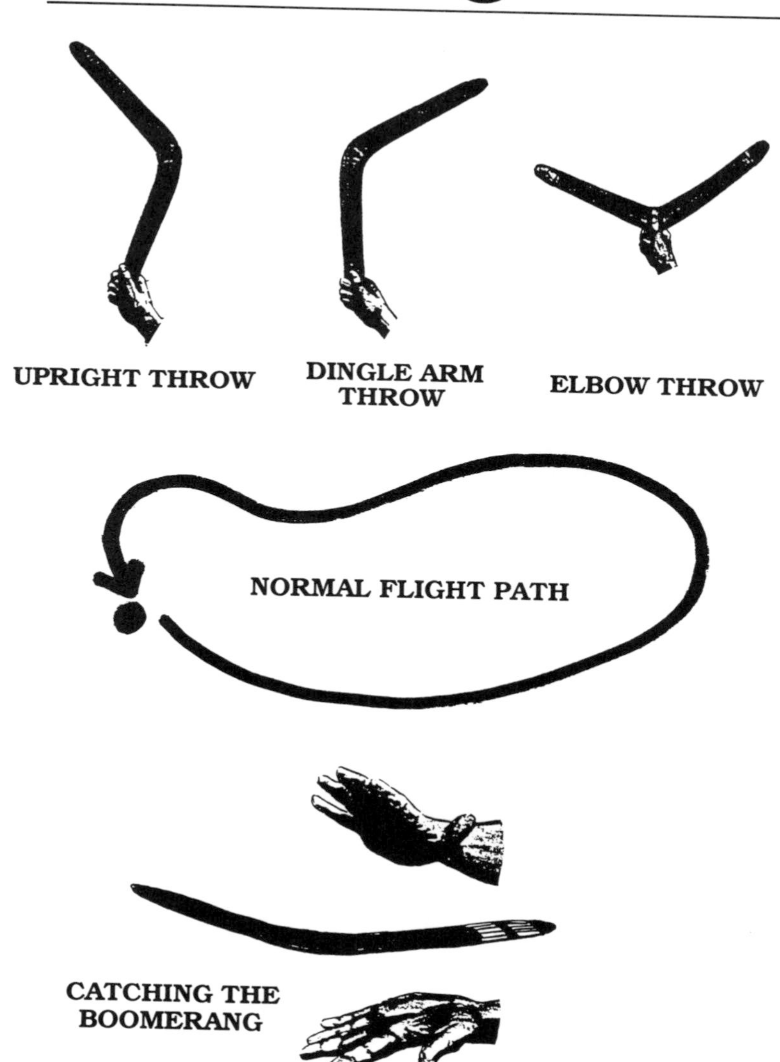

ASSOCIATED HUNTING IMPLEMENTS

OTHER IMPLEMENTS WHICH MAY BE USED IN CONJUNCTION WITH HUNTING BOOMERANGS

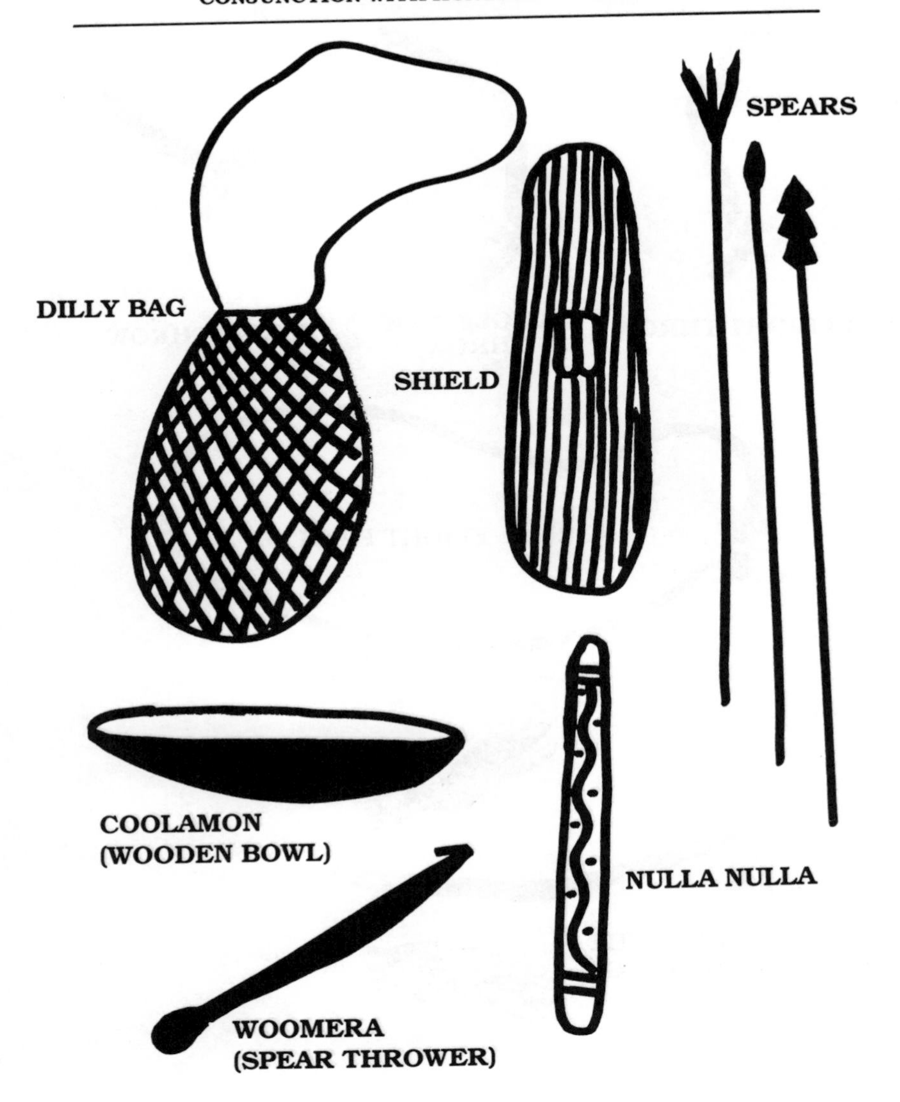